Sea Turtles

Beautiful Marine Reptiles

By Gabriella Davila

Special Thank You's

I want to thank Elisa Velasquez, thank you for believing and supporting me .I am so thankful to God for your love, support, help and motivation in helping me in my journey to help save sea life. I love you very much, Gabriella.

A very special thank you to Julie Suess for allowing me the chance to use her beautiful pictures. Julie, your pictures are amazing and thank you so much. I am so excited.

Thank you, Gabriella

Sea Turtles

Each sea turtle breed eats different kinds of food.

Did you know that Sea Turtles always cry? Because of the salt in the ocean, this causes the turtle to always cry.

Leatherback, Green, Loggerhead, Kemps Riley, Hawksbill, Olive Ridley and Flat back are the 7 types of turtles.

Sea Turtles always lay their eggs at the same beach where they were born.

Sea turtles cannot hide in their shells like land turtles can, so this many times causes them to get hurt .

Did you know that Sea turtles can sleep 2 hours without coming up for air.

\

Sea Turtles can be badly injured from boat motors, plastic, straws, balloons and other garbage.

Did you know that sea turtles have spines and ribs just like humans.

Sea turtles all have different types of jaws,
the reason for that is because each turtle
diet is very different.

I live by Hutchinson Island, Florida. Here in Hutchinson Loggerhead turtles come and lay their eggs.

Sea turtles go back and lay their eggs at the exact place they are born. Some turtles will travel many miles.

Did you know that plastic items such as straws can hurt the sea turtles?

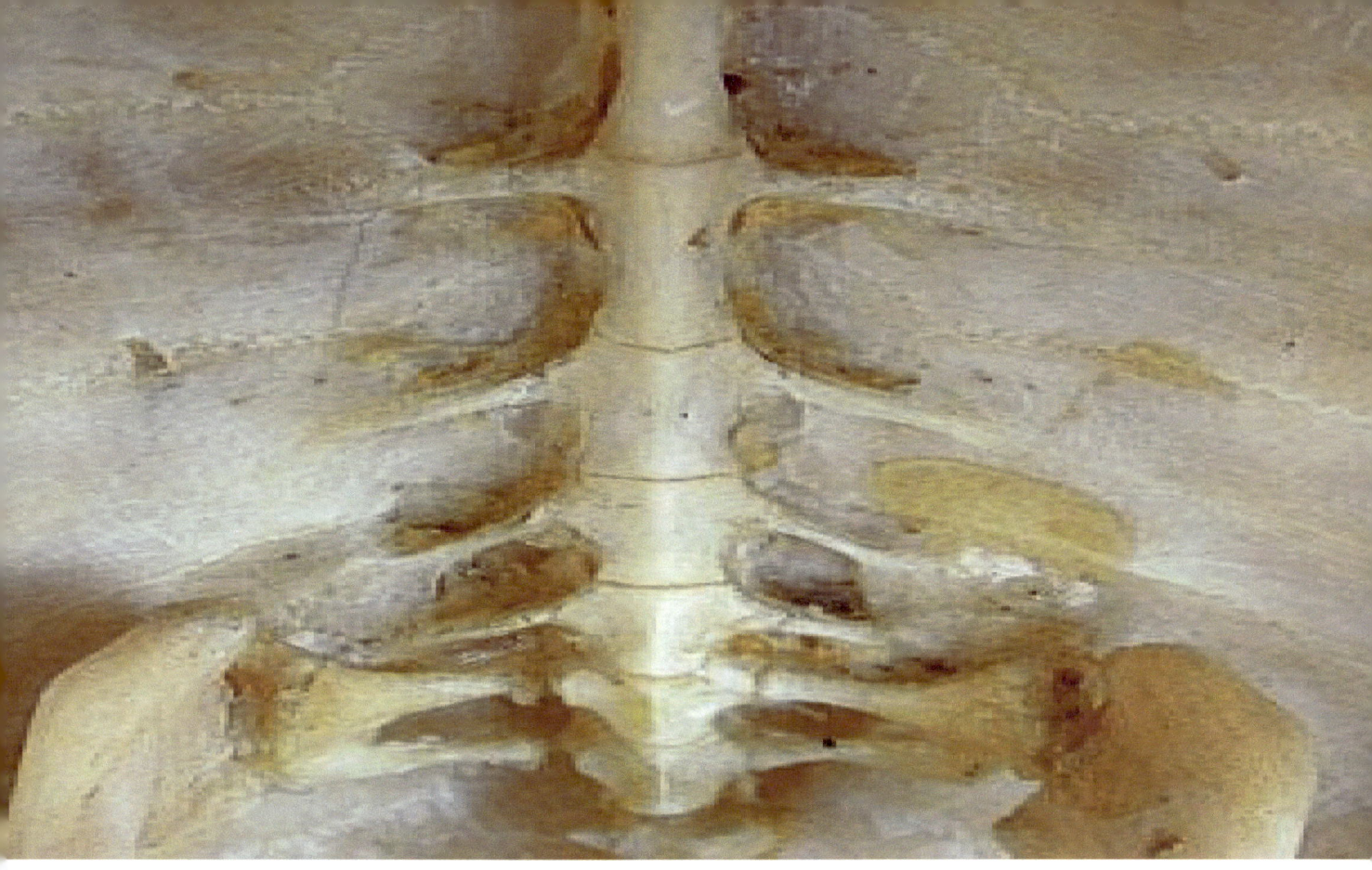

Sea turtles like humans have spines and ribs. This allows the sea turtle to swim and travel the water currents easily.

71 percent of the earth is covered in water.
14 percent of the sea life is known to
humans.

Gabriella Davila

Gabriella Davila is a 10 year author. Her love for the ocean has been something that has been an interest to her at a very young age. She loves to read, write, study and learn all she can about the Oceans. Her goal is to help people understand the importance of sea life and how important they are to the earth's foundation. Gabriella has other books that can be found on

Amazon.com/Gabriella Davila

Julie Suess

Julie Suess is one of the most dynamic underwater photographers. She is passionate lover of all sea life. Her pictures have been used in many websites, books and other publications. Julie's love for the sea turtles is truly amazing and with her eyes and camera lens, you have the ability to see the oceans most beautiful sea reptile. Julie has many beautiful photos and can be found on,

http://juliesuessphotography.smugmug.com

Dawn Davila

Dawn is Gabriella's mother who like her daughter Gabriella has a love and passion for the Ocean and the life that call the oceans home. Dawn like Julie Suess and Gabriella believes in protect every animal that calls the earth's waters home. She believes they should be respected and protect.

www.ingramcontent.com/pod-product-compliance
Lightning Source LLC
Chambersburg PA
CBHW041831280526
45792CB00006B/2057